Gymnastics

GETTING THE EDGE: CONDITIONING, INJURIES, AND LEGAL & ILLICIT DRUGS

VIRTUOSI

Gymnastics

by J. S. McIntosh

Mason Crest Publishers

VIRTUOSI

MASON CREST PUBLISHERS INC.
370 Reed Road
Broomall, Pennsylvania 19008
(866)MCP-BOOK (toll free)
www.masoncrest.com

First Printing
9 8 7 6 5 4 3 2 1

Library of Congress Cataloging-in-Publication Data

McIntosh, J. S.
  Gymnastics / by J. S. McIntosh.
    p. cm. — (Getting the edge: conditioning, injuries, and legal & illicit drugs)
  Includes bibliographical references and index.
  ISBN 978-1-4222-1734-4   ISBN (series) 978-1-4222-1728-3
  1. Gymnastics—Juvenile literature. 2. Gymnastics—Training—Juvenile literature. I. Title.
  GV461.3.M325 2011
  796.44—dc22
                                        2010010053

Produced by Harding House Publishing Service, Inc.
www.hardinghousepages.com
Interior Design by MK Bassett-Harvey.
Cover Design by Torque Advertising + Design.
Printed in the USA by Bang Printing.

The creators of this book have made every effort to provide accurate information, but it should not be used as a substitute for the help and services of trained professionals.

Contents

VIRTUOSI

Introduction

GETTING THE EDGE: CONDITIONING, INJURIES, AND LEGAL & ILLICIT DRUGS is a four-teen-volume series written for young people who are interested in learning about various sports and how to participate in them safely. Each volume examines the history of the sport and the rules of play; it also acts as a guide for prevention and treatment of injuries, and includes instruction on stretching, warming up, and strength training, all of which can help players avoid the most common musculoskeletal injuries. Each volume also includes tips on healthy nutrition for athletes, as well as information on the risks of using performance-enhancing drugs or other illegal substances. GETTING THE EDGE offers ways for readers to healthily and legally improve their performance and gain more enjoyment from playing sports. Young athletes will find these volumes informative and helpful in their pursuit of excellence.

Sports medicine professionals assigned to a sport with which they are not familiar can also benefit from this series. For example, a football athletic trainer may need to provide medical care for a local gymnastics meet. Although the emergency medical principles and action plan would remain the same, the athletic trainer could provide better care for the gymnasts after reading a simple overview of the principles of gymnastics in GETTING THE EDGE.

Although these books offer an overview, they are not intended to be comprehensive in the recognition and management of sports injuries. They should not replace the professional advice of a trainer, doctor, or nutritionist. The text helps the reader appreciate and gain awareness of the sport's history, standard training techniques, common injuries, dietary guidelines,

VIRTUOSITY

and the dangers of using drugs to gain an advantage. Reference material and directed readings are provided for those who want to delve further into these subjects.

Written in a direct and easily accessible style, GETTING THE EDGE is an enjoyable series that will help young people learn about sports and sports medicine.

—*Susan Saliba, Ph.D., National Athletic Trainers' Association Education Council*

Gymnastics

1
Overview of Gymnastics

Understanding the Words

Things that are synchronized take place at the same time.

Acrobatic has to do with performances that emphasize balance and coordination.

Eligibility has to do with being qualified for a task.

Criteria are factors used to judge a contest (for instance, a gymnastic performance).

An apparatus is a piece of equipment used to perform a task. In this book, apparatus refers to parts of the gym like parallel bars or suspended rings.

Elite means that something is intended for only the top few.

VIRTUOSI

VIRTUOSITY

Gymnastics is a sport involving exercises that require physical strength, flexibility, agility, balance, and coordination. There are different activities within gymnastics, from group activities to individual ones. The exercises also concentrate on different skills, ranging from leaping to keeping good rhythm.

Ancient History

Gymnastic sports have been around as long as or longer than any other athletic activity. They originated in ancient Greece; the philosopher Plato mentions gymnastics in his classic the *Republic*, where he stated that "gymnastics [should] be preserved in their original form and no innovation made."

> **DID YOU KNOW?**
>
> The first Olympics took place in 776 B.C.E., in Olympia, Greece. Running, however, was the only sport included.

Athletes have not listened to his advice! Gymnastics were performed quite differently in ancient Greece than they are performed currently. For example, ancient Greeks considered wrestling, running, and boxing to be a part of gymnastics; today we think of these as separate sports.

In the second century B.C.E., the Roman Empire took over Greece—and with this change in government, came major cultural shifts as well. Gymnastics changed form, losing the Greek emphasis on self-improvement, and turned into violent gladiator fights. In 393 C.E., a series of financial scandals and the rise of Christianity, which did not encourage a focus on the body's abilities, ended gymnastics until the modern era.

VIRTUOSITY

Nineteenth-Century Rebirth

Friedrich Ludwig Jahn and Per Hernrik Ling made gymnastics popular again in the nineteenth century. During the early 1800s, physical competition was popular in Europe, especially in the armed forces. Jahn, a German schoolteacher, invented the exercises and equipment that are used in modern gymnastics, including the parallel bars, vaulting horse, rings, and the horizontal bar. He organized associations called *turneveins* for the practice of gymnastics. German emigrants exported these organizations to the United States, and the *turneveins* became the foundation of modern gymnastic associations.

> **DID YOU KNOW?**
>
> *The ancient Greeks performed gymnastics naked. The word for "gymnastics" comes from two separate roots: the Greek words for "naked" and "fond of athletic exercise."*

While Friedrich Jahn developed gymnastics based on equipment; Ling developed routines based on fluid and expressive body movement without equipment. These were also known as rhythmic gymnastics.

Friedrich Ludwig Jahn is known as "Turnvater" or "Turnpater" Jahn, which roughly translates to "the father of gymnastics."

VIRTUOSITY

Across nineteenth-century Europe, gymnastics became popular in schools and sports clubs. In the United States, gymnastics were established in the 1830s, and the first official gymnastic club was founded in 1850. During this era, the Federation Internationale Gymnastique (FIG) officially controlled and regulated world gymnastics. Meanwhile, in the United Kingdom, the British Amateur Gymnastics Association (AGA) formed in 1888, in the United States, the Amateur Athletic Union (AAU) regulated gymnastics after 1883.

> **DID YOU KNOW?**
> Ancient Greek gymnasts were as concerned with developing the mind in gymnastics as the body. In fact, philosophers would meet at gymnasiums along with athletes.

In 1896, the Olympic games included gymnastics for the first time. That year, the summer Olympics were appropriately held in Athens, the place where gymnastics began. Athletes performed on the vault, pommel horse, the rings, the parallel bars, and the high bar. By 1924, Olympic gymnasts competed for individual titles in each category as well as groups. Olympic officials first included women gymnasts in 1924 but only for some team titles. Not until 1952 were women allowed to compete in an equal number of categories as male gymnasts.

Modern Gymnastics

Modern gymnastics are separated into two main categories: classic gymnastics and rhythmic gymnastics.

Classic gymnasts use the traditional equipment developed by Friedrich Jahn. For men, this includes parallel bars, high bar (sometimes called the horizontal bar), rings, pommel horse, and the vault. Floor exercises are also

The parallel bars, shown here, are adjustable so the height of the bars above the floor and distance between the bars can be set for each gymnast.

Gymnastic Events

Here is a brief overview of the major gymnastic events:

- **Floor exercises**: A gymnast performs frontward or backward acrobatic movements. There are also non-acrobatic features to a performance, such as balancing moves or jumps. Both male and female gymnasts perform floor routines.
- **Pommel horse**: This is one of the hardest gymnastic events in which to compete. A player moves in circular motion on a raised bar; only his hands may touch the bar. The pommel horse is a men's event.
- **Rings**: A gymnast uses two suspended rings, swinging and flipping into positions in which he will freeze for a moment. Difficulty of the positions is a deciding factor. This is a men's event.

used. Women compete with floor exercise, uneven bars (sometimes called asymmetric bars), beam, and vaults.

In rhythmic gymnastics, dancelike athletic routines are performed on a mat, using handheld equipment such as ribbons, balls, and hoops. The equipment helps the athlete demonstrate graceful fluid movements. Both individuals and teams compete in rhythmic gymnastics. Teams demonstrate synchronized patterns when faced against one another. Rhythmic gymnastics started in

- **Vault**: Gymnasts sprint down a runway onto a spring-board and do flips and twists in the air before landing. Both male and female gymnasts perform the vault, although the styles are slightly different for men and women.
- **Beam**: A female gymnast performs a series of flips, turns, and somersaults on a 16 foot long balance beam, before dismounting.
- **Parallel bars**: Male gymnasts do many swings on two parallel bars. There are specific guidelines to how often they can stop and the different kind of swings required.
- **High bar**: A male gymnast does many flips and jumps while swinging on a single suspended bar before dismounting.
- **Uneven bars**: A women's gymnastic event in which gymnasts do flips and swing from one bar to the other several times before dismounting.

the 1930s. The FIG accepted them in 1962, and in 1984, officials for the Olympic games also accepted them.

Gymnastic Careers

Gymnastics requires dedication in training and self-confidence when per-forming. Athletes who compete in gymnastics dedicate large portions of their life to the game. This becomes more and more true at higher levels of

VIRTUOSITY

competition. Families have been known to move miles to get to a good coach, and young gymnasts can spend more hours practicing per week than many adults do in full-time jobs.

For athletes to transform themselves from beginners to Olympic gold medalists, they must dedicate their lives to gymnastics. Few can achieve the privilege of competing on an international level, but many rewards can be achieved even if an athlete never makes it to the Olympics. Advancing to high stages of competition, such as a national team, can happen in a

DID YOU KNOW?

Women's gymnastics get more coverage and attention than men's. This is different than most team sports, especially basketball. There are a few other sports in which the sexes get equal attention (like tennis), but gymnastics is one of the few in which women's participation is more emphasized.

The two bars on the uneven bar apparatus are 4.3 ft (130cm) to 5.9 ft (180 cm) apart, depending on each gymnast's individual adjustment.

Gymnastics

DID YOU KNOW?

Female gymnasts reach their athletic peak much sooner than male gymnasts. Female gymnasts are at their best between ages 14 to 18. Male gymnasts, on the other hand, achieve peak performance in their late teens to early twenties. In 1996, the Olympics raised the minimum age for young women to perform gymnastics from fifteen to sixteen. While this doesn't seem like a dramatic change, many coaches were upset because age fifteen may be when female gymnasts are at their peak.

Artistic elements are an important part of the overall score in some of the gymnastic events. This jump is known as a "stag ring leap," and it combines athletic ability with dance-like movement.

Gymnastics

VIRTUOSITY

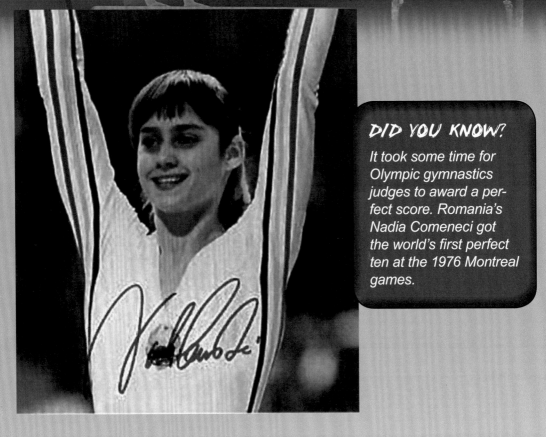

DID YOU KNOW?

It took some time for Olympic gymnastics judges to award a perfect score. Romania's Nadia Comeneci got the world's first perfect ten at the 1976 Montreal games.

much shorter time than it would in many other sports. Talent and dedication pay off.

Junior Olympic Program

The first step in the journey to becoming a national representative is getting into the Junior Olympic Program (J.O.P.) There are ten levels for girls and seven for boys. Age and ability determine the levels for boys, while ability alone determines the level for young women. Gymnasts go up the levels by

VIRTUOSITY

increasing the quality of technique in their special field. To pass the first levels, gymnasts perform techniques required by the governing body of gymnastics in the United States. In these performances, they must grade high enough to advance to the next level. At the higher levels of eligibility, the athlete can choose the technique in which he performs.

The criteria to judge each level of the J.O.P. are difficult. Any error in style or technique results in points deducted from an athlete's final score. In the men's Class 5 level of the J.O.P., gymnasts are required to achieve a score of at least 9.3 out of 10.0. The routines for men's Class 5 are: floor exercises,

DID YOU KNOW?

Most gymnasts start performing at a young age, sometimes as early as two years old. The earlier an athlete performs, the better her chances of advancing to the highest levels of competition.

Gymnastics

VIRTUOSITY

pommel horse, rings, vault, parallel bars, and the high bar. According to the rules:

> If the skills of each sequence are performed with improper technique or if this gymnast falls on or off the apparatus, has a lapse in form, or any other errors, deductions are taken.

Gymnasts make up for lost points through a "virtuosity bonus," additional points awarded for flawlessly executing a technique.

Even if it is possible to achieve a higher class in the J.O.P., it may not be the best option. When starting a new class, a gymnast may feel overwhelmed. By going into a new class too early, she may start at the bottom when she was previously very competitive at a lower level. Choosing to stay at a lower level a little longer may not be unwise.

Getting a 10.0: The Scoring System

The basic scoring is based on how many errors a competitor makes. Single deductions range from:

- 0.1 (small error)
- 0.2 (medium error)
- 0.3 (large error)
- 0.5 (fall or an added part)
- 1.0 (missing part)

VIRTUOSITY

Pommel horse routines require a lot of upper body strength, which is why they are only done by male gymnasts.

Elite Program

If a gymnast passes through the J.O.P., he is able to enter the Elite Program, also known as the International Program. This is the most intensive program, with training conducted under the eyes of the U.S.A. Gymnastics Training Team; many gymnasts train up to thirty-six hours a week. The training team picks individuals who will represent the United States in major competition. Participants in the Elite Program are eligible to compete in U.S. National Championships and in international competitions, including the Olympics and World Championships.

Gymnastics

Disagreements in Scoring

Sometimes there are disagreements among specialists between what is a fair judging call. In the 1992 Olympics, Tatiana Gutsu beat Shannon Miller by .012, which was the smallest margin of victory ever. Her win was very controversial for a number of reasons. While Miller had a relatively error-free competition, Gutsu stumbled forward in the opening of her floor routine. Adding to the outrage, Gutsu didn't qualify for the all-around competition, but her coaches pushed her into the team that was playing because they saw potential for Olympic gold from her.

At another competition, where Paul Hamm was the first American to win gold, the bronze medalist, Yang Tae-Young, claimed a judging error on his parallel bar routine docked him one-tenth of a point unfairly. The International Gymnastics Federation (FIG) agreed with Young, but because the score wasn't disputed immediately after being announced, Paul Hamm kept the trophy.

With competitions so close, the scoring and rules are up to the judges.

VIRTUOSITY

Young gymnasts who show exceptional talent can go through fast track courses such as the "Future Stars" and "Talent Opportunity Program," which consist of training and competitive events at the highest standards. Only gymnasts who meet the exacting demands of the programs are able to get into them. The Elite Program has many detailed evaluations that assess the gymnast's talent, and its leaders choose individuals to compete in the U.S. National Championships.

Olympic Glory

After the National Championships, the National Team chooses competitors for international teams. Most of those chosen are ranked winners, but not all are. Once selected, however, a gymnast does not have a guaranteed entry into the Olympics. The National Team requires an enormous amount of training, and once on the team, the athlete must continually prove her right to remain there.

Keep It Fun

The more you enjoy gymnastics the better you will be at it. Training isn't always fun and competition can be stressful, but make sure to enjoy the sport. Steve Whitlock, Director of Internet Services at USA Gymnastics, says: "the main reason why young people drop out of gymnastics is that their sport stops being fun."

VIRTUOSITY

George Eyser

Born in 1871 in Kiel, Germany, Eyser moved to Denver, Colorado, at the age of fourteen. He lost his leg after being stuck by a train, but this did not stop him from being a fierce competitor in gymnastics. He became a U.S. citizen in 1894, and in October 1904, he performed in the Olympics, winning three gold medals for the United States in one day, as well as winning two silver medals and one bronze medal. This achievement is even more incredible when you consider that disabled players competed as equals with nondisabled players!

Gymnastics

Shannon Miller

Shannon Miller has won more medals than any other gymnast in America. She was born in Oklahoma and began training at the age of five. At age nine, her family moved her to Russia for a time to train. There, Shannon impressed the Soviet trainers, who believed she had the natural potential to be a world-class gymnast. By 1991, at the Arthur Gandor competition, she achieved an all-around score of 39.875, the highest total amount of points ever recorded by an American woman within a traditional scale. She continued to win medals, eventually gaining seven Olympic gold medals and nine World Championship medals. This makes her the most decorated American gymnast, male or female, in the history of the sport. She is also the only woman—for any sport—to be inducted into the United States Olympic Hall of Fame twice. Her competitive spirit is what always kept her going. She once said, "I compete with myself"—which for the best gymnasts, is the toughest, most rigorous competition of all.

2
Mental Preparation & Safety

Understanding the Words

If someone or something is professional, *that person or thing follows the rules of behavior that apply to someone who makes her living in a particular field. A gym that is professional takes safety and sportsmanship as seriously as if each athlete training there were going on to earn his living at gymnastics.*

Visualization *is the act of making a mental picture of something.*

VIRTUOSITY

Mental preparation is crucial to success in gymnastics. If an athlete is distracted or tired, she won't be able to perform to the best of her ability. There is little to no room for error in gymnastics, so being mentally prepared before a competition is important. Lynn Jennings, an Olympic gold medalist in running, stated, "Mental will is a muscle that needs exercise, just like muscles of the body."

Finding a Gym

To be fully prepared, you need to find the right coach. Look for these qualities in the coach's gym:

- a friendly, professional atmosphere between staff and trainees

- well-kept equipment that meets the highest standards

- trainers that have a safety certification from the U.S.A. gymnastics.

- coaches that keep their athletes busy with events, competitions, and social activities.

Mental Training

The purpose of mental training is to control your inner voice, that little part of you that whispers all your worries, self-criticism, and doubts. Gymnastics take concentration and determination, and that negative inner voice can distract you. The more you can control your thoughts while you're performing, the better your chances are of excelling in gymnastics.

Try your best to control negative thoughts and push them into a positive, constructive direction. Say positive statements to yourself like, "Each day I am getting better at the high bar," even when you don't feel your best. Fake it till you make it! By repeating these statements, you encourage both your mind and your body to perform at their best. If a negative thought arises,

VIRTUOSITY

To be a successful gymnast, preparing your mind is as important as preparing your body.

Gymnastics

Mental Focus During Competition

Follow these guidelines before and during a competition to keep up your mental focus:

- Make sure every item of equipment has been packed. If you forget something you need, it increases anxiety and lowers confidence.
- Arrive at the competition on time; being late causes worry you don't need.
- Warm up in the competition hall if you can. By getting used to the environment (the noise of the crowd, lighting, etc.), you can get an advantage in competition.
- Visualize your performance before you start competing. Picture yourself with grace and confidence.
- Make sure to eat something small and high in carbohydrates before and after a competition. Food is your body's fuel.
- Keep it fun, even during a competition. Judges react well to a positive attitude—and keeping your feelings light during a competition helps release stress. By acting like a competition isn't the most important event in the history of the universe, you will improve your performance.

continue to repeat a positive statement to counteract it. Continue to do this until positive thinking becomes a habit.

If an area in your life drags you down and depresses you, speak to a coach or trainer about this problem. Chances are, if a problem affects all other areas in your life, the problem will affect your performance at the gymnasium as well. Try to solve any pressing life problems with the same energy you apply to your athletics.

Memorization

By improving your memory, you can also improve your concentration and focus. Here's an exercise that will help you.

Lay five playing cards face up and memorize the cards one at a time. Flip the cards over and take a break for five minutes. After the break, try your best to remember what is on each card. If you do well at this, then increase the number of cards. This task may seem to have nothing to do with gymnastics, but it will sharpen your focus and increase your concentration.

Breathing Exercises

By closing your eyes, you can focus your mind on your breathing. Pull air in and out of your nose and exhale out of your mouth. Be as mindful of your breathing as possible. If your mind wanders away from your breathing, bring your attention back to the sound and sensation of your lungs filling with air. Only thinking about one thing is difficult because of the way we live; we tend to multitask, with our minds racing between several things at a time. If this mental exercise is especially hard for you, don't be self-critical; simply try your best to relax and slow down your mind. These exercises need to be repeated; as with anything in life, the more you practice, the better you will get. Doing these exercise will help you be able to strengthen your concentration while performing.

VIRTUOSITY

Visualization

If you are learning a difficult maneuver, visualization may help reduce anxiety and improve performance. While sitting in a quiet, comfortable place, imagine performing the tasks that you are most worried about. Imagine all the actions that you will perform; be as detailed as possible. Picture yourself performing these actions perfectly. Think of the sound of the crowd, the silence before you start, the feeling in your muscles while you perform, the scores you will get, and the smile on your coach's face when you get that much-deserved 10.0. Research shows that when the mind imagines a scene in detail, the body learns the action as though it were actually doing it. While visualization cannot replace physical training, it will help your body remember techniques and improve your confidence. The more often you visualize the movements, the more your mind will help your body in learning a difficult task.

Goals

Before you train, set realistic but ambitious goals. Try and make the goals as specific as possible. All athletes have dreams of glory in their minds; the best have goals written on paper.

Benefits for Life

Gymnastics also has benefits outside of the gymnasium. Shannon Miller stated, "Gymnastics has helped me so much; it's taught me how to be dedicated to something, how to work hard, how to achieve my goals, also to be organized and how to try to balance my life out. I think it has helped me in school, too, because it has kept me organized and I'm always striving for a goal."

Gymnastics

VIRTUOSITY

An example of a vague goal would be: "Make my coach proud." Instead, set a goal for yourself you can measure, such as: "Get a bronze medal," "Score above an 8.0 at my next competition," or "Get accepted into a higher-class level by the next season." By creating measurable goals, you will increase the mental payoff from an achievement. Be realistic, though; ask your coach whether or not your goal is possible. Challenge yourself, but make sure your dream can be achieved. Don't set yourself up for failure!

Once you achieve your first goal, you may find that success creates more success. You'll feel like you're "on a roll," or you may feel that fate is on

A good coach will work with you on your techniques, and will teach you how to focus mentally as well.

Gymnastics

VIRTUOSITY

your side (even though it actually has nothing to do with luck). These feelings increase confidence, which gives you an added boost in competitions. Much of competition is mental; if you walk into a performance thinking you can win a perfect score, you heighten your chances of making the score.

Reading

Read as much as you can about gymnastics. Get books on everything from biographies of great gymnasts to instructional guides. By learning about your sport, you build enthusiasm for what you are doing. Treat gymnastics as much as a mental challenge as a physical one. By overcoming mental challenges, we are better equipped to control our bodies.

Safety

Maintaining gym equipment most likely won't be your responsibility if you train at a professional gym. Your coach should make sure that the equipment is

Advice for Parents

The support of parents is crucial. To go for a career in gymnastics at the highest levels, young athletes give up large parts of their childhoods to follow their dreams. Worries about failure and high expectations are normal. Parents need to support their child athletes and let them know that no matter how much they succeed or fail, they will still be loved the same. If the young athlete knows she has her parents' support no matter what, chances are she will perform better.

Gymnastics

VIRTUOSITY

Education and Gymnastics

The ancient Greek philosopher Plato stated thousands of years go that gymnastics was the best education: "Let us describe the education of men. What then is the education to be? Perhaps we could hardly find a better experience of the past that expresses the body than gymnastics. I believe in gymnastic for the body and music for the mind."

set up properly and that equipment works at its best. There are a few things, however, to keep in mind when exercising:

- Make sure floor mats are fastened tightly to the ground. Any gap between mats could cause injury.

- Check the spacing between pieces of equipment. If they are too close together, other athletes might collide with each other.

- Velcro® should be clean of lint. Remove lint with a stiff brush.

- Worn-out and damaged equipment should be taken care of properly. If you have any worry that a piece of equipment isn't safe, don't use it.

Gymnastics

3
Physical Preparation

Understanding the Words

Tendons *are the stretchy bands that hold muscles and bones together.*

Ligaments *are the strong tissues that hold bones together.*

Your hamstring *is the muscle at the back of your thigh—or the tendons at the back of your knee are also known as your hamstring.*

Efficiency *has to do with something's effectiveness or ability to achieve a purpose.*

VIRTUOSITY

Warming up before exercising is crucial. Cold muscles are injured much more easily than warm muscles. Without proper stretches, muscles, tendons, and ligaments have a greater risk of tearing or straining when under stress. A proper warm-up consists of light exercise to raise body temperature, followed by stretching.

Light Exercise

The goal of a warm-up is to raise the body temperature and loosen muscles. Light, gentle exercises are best; these preparatory exercises should not put the body under much strain. A gymnast needs to perform warm-ups specific to her sport to prevent injuries. Falls or impacts with equipment are the most common accidents that occur, resulting in acute sprains in the ankles and wrists.

Wrists

To warm up the wrists, shake them lightly and then circle the hands while keeping the forearms still. Circle in one direction for about twenty seconds and then reverse direction. Then, bend the hands backward and forward; change direction once every second for twenty seconds.

Know Your Limits

The exercises given in this chapter are merely guidelines. Modify the exercises to what suits you best. If you don't feel prepared once you are done with them, then repeat, and next time add more repetitions. The point of these exercises is to warm up your muscles.

VIRTUOSITY

Ankles

To warm up the ankles, put one hand against a wall and lift one leg from the floor. Circle the foot around, then alternate directions and feet. At the end, push and pull each ankle backward and forward. Repeat both movements about ten times.

Stretching

Stretching increases the body's ability to move by lengthening muscles. This is important because a gymnast needs to be able to move his body flexibly without risk of injury. For example, when a gymnast performs jumping splits, all the muscle groups and ligaments of the legs and hips are stretched to the fullest. If a gymnast is not flexible, the strain from this exercise may tear muscles or

Warming up your muscles is important before any physical activity, especially one like gymnastics that requires so much flexibility.

other tissues. Stretching reduces the possibility of sprain and helps sore muscles recover from previous workouts.

Trainers use hundreds of different stretches. Here are a few that apply most to a young gymnast.

RESISTANCE STRETCHING

Resistance stretching is based on the idea that a relaxed muscle stretches better than a tense muscle. Suddenly relaxing tense muscles allows for a more efficient stretch. Resistance stretching is an effective technique, but be careful not to stretch further than you should and tear or pull muscles. Be mindful of your limits when performing these techniques.

The "Contract-Relax" (CR) technique is the most common way to perform resistance stretches. These exercises are most often done with a partner. To stretch the hamstring muscles, the athlete lies on her back and places a leg on the shoulder of a partner who kneels in a supporting position. She contracts her hamstring muscles lightly, and pushes against the shoulder, holding for up to fifteen seconds. Then when she relaxes the muscles, her partner pushes his legs gently toward her face. This process should repeat, each time stretching the leg further and further.

STATIONARY STRETCHING

Stationary stretching is the most common type of stretch. It involves stretching to the point of tension and holding the position for up to ten seconds. While the muscle is stretched, it will relax and lengthen.

The side split is an example of a typical stationary stretch. The athlete lowers his torso toward the ground, supporting his body weight on his hands

> **DID YOU KNOW?**
>
> *Ballistic stretches are performed with bouncing or jerking movements. Most trainers today discourage this technique because sudden movements can result in damaged muscles or ligaments. These stretches also do not build flexibility in a safe or gradual manner.*

VIRTUOSITY

and opening his legs to an "A" shape. When he senses he has reached the limit of his stretch, he stops and relaxes the leg muscles for ten seconds. The athlete should then push the stretch further, holding the stretch in place for longer before gently pulling out of the position when done.

RULES FOR SAFE STRETCHING

- If you feel any sudden pain or burning sensations, stop immediately.

- Stop if you feel nauseated, faint, or ill.

- Muscles need a good supply of oxygen while stretching, so make an effort to breathe deeply and frequently.

- Stretch after a workout. Tired and sore muscles recover more quickly if stretched while the body cools down. Stretching after also prevents the body from over-tightening and stiffening.

When stretching, movements should be slow—each stretching pose should be held long enough to allow the tense muscles time to relax and lengthen.

Gymnastics

VIRTUOSITY

WHEN NOT TO STRETCH

Do not performing stretches if:

- You have a muscle injury.

- You are recovering from a bone fracture, unless stretching is a part of your physical therapy.

- After you stretch you find yourself less flexible; this could indicate a problem such as a disease or illness.

- Your joint is unstable from an injury.

- You feel intense pain when trying to stretch.

DID YOU KNOW?

Gymnasts use chalk to absorb sweat from the hands. Chalk gives the hands better grip on the rings, bars, and pommel horse. Any major gym will have chalk available. Always use chalk before mounting equipment.

Gymnastics

Safe Training

To be physically prepared, a gymnast should closely follow her coach's advice. Here are a few safety guidelines for training:

- A spotter should be present while you work out. The spotter's job is to watch and guide during techniques. Sometimes he helps by physically guiding you. Other times he will help you train by giving verbal advice.

- Use any safety apparatus while learning potentially dangerous techniques.

- While learning the vault or any other exercise that involves heavy landing, use a deep foam pad that catches your fall. You can go from softer to harder surfaces until you are ready to compete.

Training Techniques

PLANCHE STRENGTH

The planche is a position where the athlete holds her body parallel to the ground by using only her hands. The position sometimes looks as thought the athlete is floating. The gymnasts who have the most planche strength usually have an advantage over other gymnasts who don't.

Bench presses are one of the best exercises used to achieve planche strength. Do at least three sets of eight repetitions,

During training, gymnasts need to build strength to allow them to do difficult routines safely. Doing handstands or planche strength exercises will help build the necessary upper body and arm strength.

VIRTUOSITY

doing as many as possible while still being able to do the required number of repetitions comfortably. Never go beyond what you feel comfortable doing.

Dumbbell raises are also a good way to achieve strength. Raise dumbbells in each hand over your head, and then lower them slowly. Repeat eight times, doing three sets. While doing this exercise, be mindful of how straight your back is. When you do a workout, you want to isolate the muscle being used as much as possible.

Strength in your lower stomach is also important. You can work those muscles on the high bar that is used during competitions. By hanging with your wrists facing forward, bring your legs up straight. Do three sets of thirty repetitions. If this becomes easy, then you can use ankle weights.

FLEXIBILITY EXERCISES

Acrobatic exercises and dynamic movements are needed in most gymnastic exercises, so stretching is crucial. The hamstring stretch, squats, and arm rotator stretch are the major stretches needed. For the hamstring stretch, stand with a foot raised on a table. Keeping the leg bent, lean your chest toward your bent knee. You should feel your hamstring muscles tensing up. Continue and release, doing this as many time as it takes for your hamstrings to feel looser.

To perform a leg squat, stand with your feet apart. With one leg pointed forward, squat down to that leg far enough so that you can put a hand on the ground.

For an arm-up rotator stretch, you need to stand straight with arms out. Place your forearm straight upward, placing a broomstick in your hand and below your elbow; using the broom, lightly rotate the arm muscles by making rotating motions toward the wall behind you. (You don't have to necessarily use a broom; you could also use a towel or resistance band.)

Gymnastics

Practice Safety During Practice

The majority of sports injuries do not occur during performances or competitions. Sixty percent of all sports-related injuries occur during practice.

In a study in 1998, researchers found that more than 25,000 children and adolescents ages 5 to 14 went to hospital emergency rooms because of a gymnastics-related injury. Girls are especially vulnerable to injuries because of the amount of competition involved at a young age.

Gymnastics injuries are common in children and adolescents. In fact, among girls' sports, gymnastics has one of the highest injury rates for girls ages 5 to 14.

VIRTUOSITY

WEIGHT TRAINING

Some gymnasts do weight training like push-ups or bench-presses to increase upper-arm strength. The exercises used in gymnastics vary widely; for instance, a woman performing graceful gymnastic movements won't need

A successful training program has to include a lot of practice on the individual pieces of equipment. A gymnast has to memorize his routine and get his body used to all the moves before he will be prepared for competition.

Gymnastics

Dangers of Plyometrics

Young teens should beware of overdoing plyometrics. Because their muscles are still developing, injuries are a greater danger for younger athletes. Heavy plyometrics should not be practiced until an athlete is at least sixteen years old—and even then, also work with a coach to make sure you perform plyometrics correctly. Bad form can create overuse injuries that are discussed in the next chapter.

the same upper-body strength that a male gymnast does who uses immense amounts of arm strength on the pommel horse or rings.

To get increased arm strength, you can go to the weight room about three times a week to supplement your regular exercise schedule. As you go up in class rank you may need to go to the weight room more often, but at lower levels keep the gym exercises as your main source of exercise.

PLYOMETRIC TRAINING

Plyometric exercises are designed to increase muscle reaction time; they produce fast movements that produce a great amount of power. Plyometrics can also improve muscle efficiency. Think of these exercises as improving the delivery system for muscles, while other weight-training exercises improve the amount that can be delivered.

For some acrobatic exercises, plyometric training is incredibly important. The speed and power of a gymnast's muscles are put to the test more than in other sports. A good example is the vault, in which the athlete is judged by an incredibly rapid spurt of movements, which take place only in a matter of seconds.

An athlete should be careful, however, not to do too many preparatory exercises involving plyometrics. By their nature, these exercises involve breaking down the body to train it to react faster the next time. It is best to perform these exercises before the body has suffered from fatigue. Space major plyometric exercises to an every-other-day basis.

Plyometric techniques vary; we will only highlight the most useful ones for gymnastics. The broad jump, for example, improves muscle reaction time in the thighs, resulting in an ability to move the muscles in explosive spurts. Place your feet a shoulder's length apart, then crouch down very low and

Are You at Risk?

If you fall under these categories you may want to place extra attention on safety precautions:

- **performing at an advanced level**: If you are perform-ing at a high level of competitive class, especially on a national or international level, you are more at risk of injury.
- **doing your main exercises on the beam**: Falls are common.
- **practicing more than 20 hours a week**: Athletes who practice this much need to be very mindful of overuse injuries (highlighted in the next chapter)

VIRTUOSITY

Using the Internet

Like nearly every other topic, there is a great wealth of information about gymnastics on the Internet, with thousands of links to all aspects of the sport. Keep in mind that nothing can beat the advice of a personal trainer. While the Internet is a great source of information once you have a background in gymnastics, it can have misleading or sometimes false information. Beware of what you read and always consult with your trainer before trying a new exercise.

extend your legs to do a jump. Jump by swinging your arms while bending your knees to increase distance. Measure the distance you covered and aim to improve it next time. The broad jump puts a larger amount of strain on your body than other exercises, so it is called a high-impact exercise.

Simpler, lower-impact exercises can also improve muscle reaction time. An example is the ankle bounce: an athlete rapidly bounces on her feet without any pause. This exercise should isolate the muscles around the ankle, improving reaction time.

Gymnastics

4
Common Injuries, Treatment, & Recovery

Understanding the Words

Inflammation *is when body tissue reacts to injury or stress by becoming hot and swollen.*

A dislocation *happens when a body part is pushed out of its normal position.*

Alignment *means that things are lined up correctly.*

Immobilizes *means to make something so that it cannot move.*

A regimen *is a course of physical training.*

Mobility *is the ability to move.*

A diagnosis *is an identification of the source of a physical problem.*

VIRTUOSITY

There are two types of injury common to gymnastics: injuries from falling or hitting an object, and slow wear-and-tear that finally results in an injured joint or limb. Both types happen equally as much.

The most typical injuries that occur are sprains, muscle strains, bruises, and inflammation. Parts of the body that are easily damaged differ between men and women. Female athletes most frequently injure their feet, ankles, knees, hands, wrists, and elbows, while male gymnasts can also suffer these injuries, but their backs and shoulders are injured more often than women's. The reason men suffer these injuries more is because the parallel bars, rings, and pommel horse all put emphasis on the back and shoulders; women don't use these apparatus.

Sprains

When a joint twists in the wrong direction, a sprain occurs. The athlete will feel pain and tenderness in the effected area, and the joint can appear swollen and bruised. When sprained, the joint will not be able to move as well. The more often a sprain occurs, the more serious the damage is to the ligament, and the worse the swelling will look. The pain from a sprained joint can last for years. The knees and wrists are the most common parts of the body to suffer from sprains.

DID YOU KNOW?

If you've suffered from an injury, your chances of being injured again are much greater. A coach should carefully monitor a previously injured athlete.

When a sprain occurs:

• Stop using the joint.

• Rest the damaged joint in a position that is comfortable, supporting it with a cushion.

VIRTUOSITY

- Use a cold compress (a bag of ice or cold water) on the swollen joint. This will reduce further swelling.

- Wrap the joint in soft padding and bandage it in place. You could also use a compression bandage, which holds the injured area tightly.

- If an ankle is severely damaged, raise the leg on a chair to reduce blood flow and lessen swelling.

These are treatments that need to be used immediately after the joint has been sprained. After these things have been done, the injured athlete may need medical treatment. Treatment will involve physical therapy and in some extreme cases, surgery.

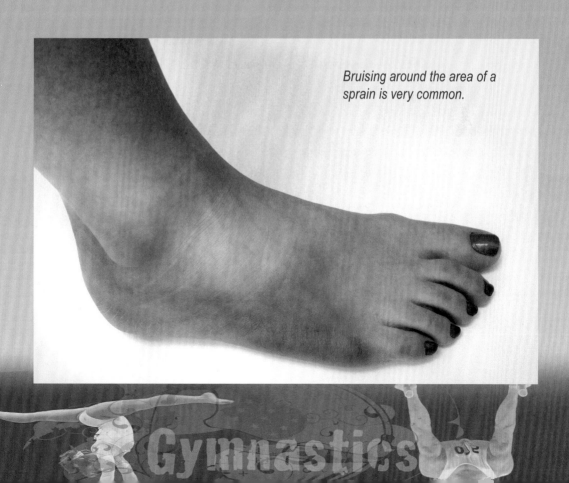

Bruising around the area of a sprain is very common.

Gymnastics

VIRTUOSITY

Degrees of Pain

When you are injured think about what kind of pain you are going through. Is it acute or chronic? Acute pain occurs with a sharp, sudden sensation that is located in one location in the body, while chronic pain occurs gradually and feels like a dull ache.

For sprains, rest is usually the best medicine. If you know you have a sprain, refrain from any strenuous activity for a week or longer. The cold compress should be applied a few times daily, but try not to apply it to your body for more than twenty minutes at a time, since localized frostbite may occur if it's applied any longer.

After a week of rest, begin to move the joint around, gently testing your joint's range of movement (R.O.M.). An example of testing your R.O.M. would be to slowly rotate a sprained ankle, reversing directions after a few light turns. The goal in doing an exercise like this is to make the joint flexible again. If any pain occurs, stop moving the joint and go back to earlier steps. After the joint can fully move in all directions, use lightweight exercises to strengthen it.

A sprain can take from one week to two months to heal. Go back to training gradually, and stay mindful of the injured joint. If the sprain still hurts after six months, go back to your doctor.

DID YOU KNOW?

Younger athletes are less likely to injure themselves than older ones. Children do not have the strength in their muscle to cause the overuse injury or accidents that are common to older teens in gymnastics. As a teen gets older and grows muscle mass, he needs increased attention and education about sports injuries.

Gymnastics

VIRTUOSITY

The treatments highlighted here for sprains can also be used for pulled muscles, pulled ligaments, or bruising. Specialists call these "soft-tissue" injuries. Most injuries that cause swelling and bruising and amounts of pain that are not very severe can be treated in a similar manner: apply a cold compress, rest, and if needed, raise the limb.

Don't self-diagnose a serious medical problem. If at any time you feel an unusual amount of pain, consult a doctor or paramedic. Always let your coach know what you are going through. A coach should have experience with how to prevent and treat different kinds of injuries.

Fractures and Dislocations

When the force of impact on a bone is too much for it to handle, it breaks. A fracture occurs when a bone is broken into pieces or snaps due to high stress

A broken bone may need to be held immobile through the use of a hard cast. This allows the bones to heal without risk of further injury.

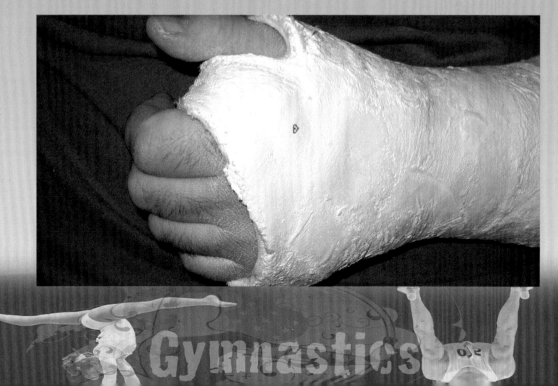

VIRTUOSITY

from impact. When a knee or shoulder is pushed out of its normal position, a dislocation occurs. In gymnastics, fractures and dislocations are rarer than in sports that are higher impact.

Gymnasts do, however, sometimes suffer these injuries. A fracture can occur in the legs and arms or wrist and fingers from a heavy fall from a piece of equipment or a bad landing from a vault jump. Dislocations usually occur in the knees from heavy falls or landings. The shoulders and fingers are damaged from accidents on the pommel horse, rings, or parallel bars.

Fractures require direct medical attention. Good gyms have at least one employee available who is trained in first-aid, but any break requires hospital treatment. In a hospital setting, treatments vary according to degree of the injury. A common treatment is called a "reduction," where a doctor places a bone back in its correct alignment. Doctors also can place limbs in a cast,

The most common wrist injury in gymnastics is a dorsal wrist impingement, which occurs when the back of the radius (one of the lower arm bones) strikes the wrist bones. This injury is aggravated whenever the body's full weight is placed on the wrist.

VIRTUOSITY

which temporarily immobilizes the injured area. Immobilization causes the range of motion to be limited; the cast ensures that no further injury can occur and that the bones can grow back together. In some extreme cases, a doctor may need to perform surgery. In surgery, parts of the bone are rearranged using screws or metal plates. An external frame is placed around the wound. Sometimes metal bars will be used to connect surgical pins and screws that will hold the fractured bones together, creating greater stability while the bone heals.

RETURNING TO TRAINING

After a fracture has been reduced and immobilized, the body can now begin to heal itself naturally. The doctor will decide when a cast, brace, or frame can be removed. At that point, gentle training can resume. Caution is required because muscles, ligaments, and bones weaken through lack of use. If a gymnast continues where she left off before the fracture, she will stress the injured area and likely cause a re-injury. Instead of going fully back into an exercise regimen, gradually increase pressure on the fractured limb over a period of weeks. Continue to do this until the bone is back to its normal form.

HEALING DISLOCATIONS

A doctor relocates a joint to a normal position after a dislocation. Similar techniques are used as after a fracture: the joint is temporarily immobilized. The healing time depends on the amount of damage to the ligament or muscles. The athlete should begin light exercises after four to six weeks of total inaction.

Gymnastics

VIRTUOSITY

Younger athletes are more vulnerable to a re-dislocation after the first injury. Damaged ligaments are easily weakened or stretched back to the first dislocation. Eight-five percent of athletes ages sixteen to twenty-five will suffer another dislocation at a later date.

Recovery for an athlete can take several months. Surgery may be needed to prevent re-injury. After medical attention, dislocations require gradual recovery. Make sure not to overload during training until the dislocated ligament is more flexible.

Overuse Injury

Half of all gymnastic injuries are caused by accidents, which happen suddenly. The other half of all injuries are caused by a gradual weakening of muscles, ligament, bone, or joint. These injuries are harder to detect and require more attention from the athlete. It is clear when a bone is broken; it is harder to stop an overuse injury before the problem becomes unbearable. Because of this, be conscious of these warning signs that indicate that a body part is injured or will be injured soon:

- stiffness when exercising a joint

- ongoing pain in muscle or joint

- decreased ability to stretch

- reduction in mobility of limbs.

- weakness in a particular body area

- inflammation in a joint or a muscle.

- uneven movements in a joint

DID YOU KNOW?

A great way to ensure that you are avoiding overuse injury but are staying fit and active is to try another sport. Dr. George C. Branche III recommends, "If you're playing different sports you learn to exercise muscles differently, you get a different training regimen and [chronic injuries are] less likely to happen." Try to keep the other sport you practice as fun as possible. Don't worry as much about winning or losing but rather on working out other areas of the body that you might not always use.

VIRTUOSITY

If any of these symptoms are severe, consult your coach or a doctor. Honesty is important: explain exactly how you feel. Do not put up with any pressure from anyone to continue training if you feel the symptoms listed above. If any coach or other authority figure pressures you to continue performing, this is a sign that person shouldn't be in charge of your gymnastics career!

A minor ache that is not treated can easily turn into a painful injury. Do not ignore a buildup of pain.

PREVENTING AND HEALING OVERUSE INJURIES

While no single event causes an overuse injury, these injuries should be taken as seriously as a heavy fall or a bad landing.

The single most important element of healing an overuse injury is rest. If the pain is bad enough, stop training altogether. If the injury is in one specific location, or localized, a gymnast can stop exercising only in that one location. If an athlete is in severe pain, she can use ice to reduce discomfort or stop swelling. A doctor can recommend a specific exercise plan to rehabilitate the injured body part. Once the problem is addressed, stretching and strengthening exercises build muscles back to their former state. For dislocated joints, wear a support while healing and during future gymnastic activities.

The start of an overuse injury could be normal wear-and-tear from gymnastics, but it could also be caused by incorrect techniques. Specific techniques for almost all gymnastics are for the benefit of the athlete's health. A few examples of incorrect techniques that can cause overuse injuries are:

• ankle problems from incorrect foot alignment

• a knee injury from landing incorrectly on vaults or dismounting from equipment

Gymnastics

VIRTUOSITY

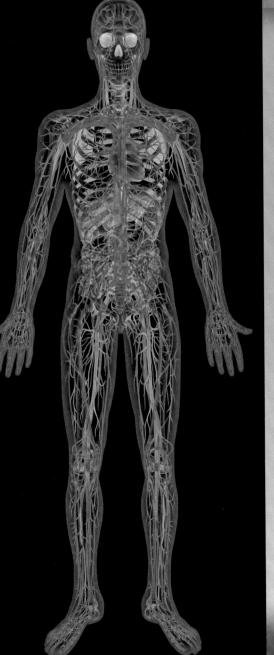

Potential overuse injuries can easily be prevented.

Back Injuries

Due to the amount of flexibility involved, gymnasts are more at risk for back injuries than other athletes. Young female gymnasts are most vulnerable because their movements often involve curving their back, which can damage the spine. Female gymnasts between twelve and eighteen should be mindful of lower back pain; if pain continues, there is a 25 percent chance of a lower-back fracture or stress fracture. All gymnasts should be aware of these symptoms:

• a painful ache in the lower back after a training session is completed

• pain in the back or legs

• reduced mobility in the back, which prevents twisting or bending

• a tingling, numb sensation in the arms or legs

Pain, tingling, or numbness in the legs can be a sign of a spinal injury. These feelings are caused when the spinal nerves that carry information between the spinal cord and the legs are damaged or pinched.

VIRTUOSITY

If any of these symptoms occur, consult your coach or doctor as soon as possible. A spine-damage injury could result in the athlete having to give up gymnastics. If there is a risk that spine damage has occurred, exercise should stop until a doctor gives a full diagnosis. For the doctor to identify the source of the back problem, she may x-ray or scan bones.

If a back issue occurs, a doctor could recommend exercises to keep back muscles flexible and reduce tightening. The movements that caused the injury may need to be removed from the routine. A potential back injury does not have to be the end of a gymnastics career, however; it could simply be a sign that more caution is needed.

The risk of lower back injury for adolescents is highest during vigorous training where the body becomes too fatigued to allow for proper protection to the back. Incorrect movement techniques, weak stomach muscles, and poor leg stamina are some of the common causes of injuries.

Gymnastics

5
Nutrition and Supplements

Understanding the Words

A nutritionist *is someone who specializes in helping people eat healthy diets.*

Moderation *means in the middle—not too much, not too little.*

Synthesis *means the process of putting something together.*

Something that is fortified *is made stronger than it would have been otherwise.*

Body image *is a person's idea of how his or her body looks.*

An eating disorder *is a psychiatric condition where a person's eating habits are not based on health or nutrition but rather the person's perception that she is too fat (regardless of how thin she may actually be). Anorexia is an eating disorder that causes people to starve themselves, while bulimia is another eating disorder that causes people to binge, eating huge quantities of food, and then purge themselves by making themselves throw up.*

Arbitrary *has to do with something that is based on no good reason.*

Portrayals *are depictions of a person or group of people.*

A pandemic *is a disease or disorder that affects large areas of the planet.*

VIRTUOSITY

You've probable heard someone say, "You are what you eat." As trite as it may sound, it's true. Although practice and training are important parts of being safe and successful in gymnastics, you also need to think about what you take into your body. Athletes must be careful to eat a proper blend of nutrients to make sure their bodies and minds perform as well as they possibly can. This doesn't just mean eating healthy foods but also choosing when to eat, how much to eat, and whether to take dietary supplements. Of course, when you choose a new diet or supplements, you should consult with a nutritionist, doctor, or some other expert. Don't make up your own nutrition program!

What to Eat

While a balanced diet is important for everyone, it is even more important for athletes. Typically, an athlete has to eat considerably more than other people

Daily caloric requirements depend on your age, sex, and activity level. Athletes, in general, need more calories per day than non athletes.

Gender	Age	Activity Level		
		Sedentary	Moderately Active	Active
Child	2–3	1,000	1,000–1,400	1,000–1,400
Female	4–8	1,200	1,400–1,600	1,400–1,800
	9–13	1,600	1,600–2,000	1,800–2,200
	14–18	1,800	2,000	2,400
	19–30	2,000	2,000–2,200	2,400
	31–50	1,800	2,000	2,200
	51+	1,600	1,800	2,000–2,200
Male	4–8	1,400	1,400–1,600	1,600–2,000
	9–13	1,800	1,800–2,200	2,000–2,600
	14–18	2,200	2,400–2,800	2,800–3,200
	19–30	2,400	2,600–2,800	3,000
	31–50	2,200	2,400–2,600	2,800–3,000
	51+	2,000	2,200–2,400	2,400–2,800

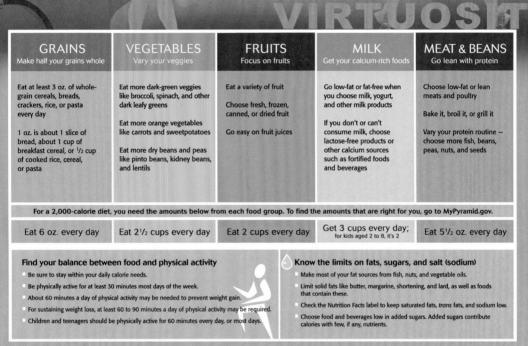

GRAINS Make half your grains whole	VEGETABLES Vary your veggies	FRUITS Focus on fruits	MILK Get your calcium-rich foods	MEAT & BEANS Go lean with protein
Eat at least 3 oz. of whole-grain cereals, breads, crackers, rice, or pasta every day 1 oz. is about 1 slice of bread, about 1 cup of breakfast cereal, or ½ cup of cooked rice, cereal, or pasta	Eat more dark-green veggies like broccoli, spinach, and other dark leafy greens Eat more orange vegetables like carrots and sweetpotatoes Eat more dry beans and peas like pinto beans, kidney beans, and lentils	Eat a variety of fruit Choose fresh, frozen, canned, or dried fruit Go easy on fruit juices	Go low-fat or fat-free when you choose milk, yogurt, and other milk products If you don't or can't consume milk, choose lactose-free products or other calcium sources such as fortified foods and beverages	Choose low-fat or lean meats and poultry Bake it, broil it, or grill it Vary your protein routine — choose more fish, beans, peas, nuts, and seeds

For a 2,000-calorie diet, you need the amounts below from each food group. To find the amounts that are right for you, go to MyPyramid.gov.

| Eat 6 oz. every day | Eat 2½ cups every day | Eat 2 cups every day | Get 3 cups every day;
for kids aged 2 to 8, it's 2 | Eat 5½ oz. every day |

Find your balance between food and physical activity
- Be sure to stay within your daily calorie needs.
- Be physically active for at least 30 minutes most days of the week.
- About 60 minutes a day of physical activity may be needed to prevent weight gain.
- For sustaining weight loss, at least 60 to 90 minutes a day of physical activity may be required.
- Children and teenagers should be physically active for 60 minutes every day, or most days.

Know the limits on fats, sugars, and salt (sodium)
- Make most of your fat sources from fish, nuts, and vegetable oils.
- Limit solid fats like butter, margarine, shortening, and lard, as well as foods that contain these.
- Check the Nutrition Facts label to keep saturated fats, *trans* fats, and sodium low.
- Choose food and beverages low in added sugars. Added sugars contribute calories with few, if any, nutrients.

This chart, from the food pyramid at MyPyramid.gov, offers dietary advice for a 2,000-calorie diet. Go to the website to find more personalized and useful information on calorie requirements and healthy diet choices.

do. The United States Food and Drug Administration (FDA) suggests that the average American should eat about 2000 calories a day; for a male high school- or college-level athlete, a 3000–4000 calorie diet is more common. There are three main food groups to consider when choosing a diet: carbohydrates, protein, and fats.

CARBOHYDRATES

Carbohydrates are foods rich in a chemical called starch, which is what the body breaks down to get energy. Starchy foods include breads and grains, vegetables such as potatoes, cereal, pasta, and rice. Roughly half an athlete's calories should

DID YOU KNOW?

Most citrus foods are high in vitamin C—so a smart move when eating lunch would be to drink orange juice along with fish or red meat. Doing this will maximize your body's ability to process the iron.

come from carbohydrates, but you should beware of heavily processed carbohydrates such as sugary foods and white bread made with bleached flour. These foods are quickly broken down into sugars, which the body processes into fats if it does not immediately burn them off. The best carbohydrate choices for an athlete are pasta and whole-grain foods, as well as starchy vegetables, which have vitamins as well as carbohydrates. A balanced diet avoids the "empty calories" supplied by white bread and sugars. Around 55 percent of a young athlete's diet—a little more than half—should be in carbohydrates.

DID YOU KNOW?

Although vitamin C will help you absorb both iron and calcium better, if you eat calcium and iron together, they will interfere with your body's ability to absorb each of them.

Pasta is a good source of carbohydrates—choose a whole grain variety and eat it with some fresh vegetable for a healthy meal.

VIRTUOSITY

Meat and eggs are good sources of protein, but should not be the only proteins you eat. Fish, nuts, and seeds should also be included because they contain protein as well as healthy fats. Cheese, which has protein, but also may be high in fat, should be eaten moderately.

PROTEIN

Proteins are important chemicals found in all living things; these chemicals are used to perform specific functions inside our body cells. Each protein is a long, folded, chain-like molecule made up of "links" called amino acids. Our bodies can break down proteins that are found in foods into their base amino acids and use them to build new proteins that make up our muscles and bones. For this reason, during any exercise regimen, it is important to eat enough protein to give the body the building blocks it needs to become stronger. The best sources of proteins are meats and dairy products (such as milk or cheese), as well as eggs and certain vegetables (such as soy, beans, and rice). A good rule of thumb for how much protein

DID YOU KNOW?

To stay healthy and fit, a man may consume thousands more calories than a woman will. Also most men's activities have a greater emphasis on arm strength and planche strength. Because of this, a diet richer in proteins and carbohydrates is needed for a man. Women who are involved in gymnastics put more emphasis on following a low-calorie diet.

Gymnastics

VIRTUOSITY

to eat is that the number of grams should be equal to about one-third of your body weight in pounds. For example, a 200-pound person should eat at least 60 or 70 grams of protein every day, or a 120-pound person should have roughly 40 grams of protein.

FATS

Lots of times, we think of fats as bad for us, since eating too much of them is unhealthy. However, fat is an important ingredient needed to make our bodies work correctly. Without fats, our bodies cannot absorb certain vitamins as well. Also, our skin and hair need some amount of fat to grow correctly. However, fats should still be eaten in moderation—no more than 70 grams a day. The

DID YOU KNOW?

The U.S. government has created a new food pyramid to help us better understand healthy nutrition. Instead of the old pyramid's emphasis on food arranged as a hierarchy, with one stacked up onto the other, the new pyramid emphasizes variety. Exercise is also part of the new pyramid, with a person walking up a set of stairs next to the pyramid.

Cholesterol

A lot of bad things have been said about cholesterol—but most of this bad press is focused on LDLs, or low-density lipoproteins, which are a kind of cholesterol that can clog our blood vessels and make our hearts work harder. Our bodies make this cholesterol out of saturated fats, such as those found in animal fat from meats, butter, and whole milk. However, there is a kind of cholesterol known as HDLs, or high-density lipoproteins, which have a good effect on the body. Increasing your HDL levels can be as easy as exercising regularly.

A healthy diet should include a lot of whole grains, vegetables, fruits, and lean protein, but very few sugars and fats.

best sources of fat are vegetable oils, olive oil, and nuts. Many foods contain saturated fats, which lead to the formation of cholesterol and can force your heart to work harder.

MINERALS

While all the major minerals are good for athletes, an athlete should make sure to consume two minerals in particular: calcium and iron. These two are also some of the minerals most likely to be under-consumed by a young athlete.

Calcium is important to strengthen bones. It is especially needed for younger athletes whose bones are still developing. Unfortunately, the body often absorbs calcium poorly; usually, only 20 percent of the calcium in a diet is consumed from the original food. Drinking lots of milk with calcium-rich

VIRTUOSITY

Staying Hydrated

The best diet in the world is no good if you become dehydrated. Dehydration occurs when your body doesn't have enough water, leading to fatigue, dizziness, and headaches, all of which can hurt your performance when playing. It's best to carry a bottle of water with you for the whole day before a practice or game to make sure that you are fully hydrated. In addition, you should be drinking water throughout the game to avoid becoming dehydrated as you sweat. Staying fully hydrated has many benefits besides helping your performance in the game—it can help mental concentration, improves digestive health, and reduces the risk of kidney stones.

cereal is best. Cheese is also an easy source to include as a snack or in a sandwich. Eating foods that contain vitamin C will also help you absorb calcium better.

Iron is another mineral needed to keep a gymnast healthy. Red meat and fish, as well as tofu and black-eyed peas, are all foods that are heavy in iron. Eating foods that are rich in vitamin C will also help your body absorb iron better.

Dietary Supplements

Many athletes seek to improve their performance by taking dietary supplements, which are pills or drinks that contain nutrients or chemicals to improve their physical health or performance in the game. Dietary supplements do not

VIRTUOSITY

include illegal performance-enhancing drugs. Instead, they contain vitamins and minerals, or chemicals that help the body use vitamins more efficiently. Although when properly used, supplements can improve overall health and performance, you should always consult a doctor or some other expert before taking them. Some examples of common supplements include vitamin tablets, creatine, and protein shakes/powder.

Everyone knows that milk is a good source of calcium, but it is not the only one. Many other foods can be excellent sources of this essential mineral.

Food	Milligrams of Calcium
Yogurt, fat-free plain (1 cup)	452
Soy beverage with added calcium (1 cup)	368
Orange juice with added calcium (1 cup)	351
Fruit yogurt, low-fat (1 cup)	345
Cheese (e.g., low-fat or fat-free American, 2 oz., about 3 slices)	323
Milk, fat-free (1 cup)	306
Milk, 1% low-fat (1 cup)	290
Tofu, firm, with added calcium sulfate (1/2 cup)	253
Cheese pizza (1 slice)*	182
Bok choy, boiled (1 cup)	158
Spinach, cooked from frozen (1 cup)**	146
Soybeans, cooked (1 cup)	130
Frozen yogurt, soft-serve vanilla (1/2 cup)	103
Macaroni and cheese (1 cup)*	92
Almonds (1 oz.)	70
Broccoli, cooked (1 cup, chopped)	62
Tortillas, flour (7")	58
Broccoli, raw (1 cup, chopped)	43
Tortillas, corn (6")	42

Gymnastics

VIRTUOSITY

VITAMIN TABLETS

For many reasons, we do not always get the vitamins and nutrients we need. Often, this is because our diets are not as balanced as they should be. Sometimes, it is because the foods that are available to us have been processed in such a way that they lose nutrients. Also, exhausted soil all over the country means that fruits and vegetables are often not as nutrient-rich as they should be. In many cases, we can get the vitamins we need from vitamin supplements. These supplements, which are usually taken as a pill, sometimes contain a balanced mixture of vitamins and nutrients (known as a multivitamin), and sometimes they contain a single vitamin or mineral that our diet is lacking. It is possible to overdose on certain vitamins, however, so be careful when taking vitamin supplements. Don't assume that because a

You should check with your doctor before starting on a multivitamin because it can be dangerous to take too much of certain vitamins.

Avoid Eat These Foods

- Fast-food/snack food: many of these snacks are high in fat but empty in calories. Foods like potato chips or french fries provide next to no dietary benefit and can do quite a lot of damage during training.
- Foods that are high in sugar. The delicious taste does not make up for the effects they cause. These "empty calories" do not enrich the body while they needlessly add to the fat and calorie count.
- Needless additives such as sugar or salt. Always choose the less fatty/sugar-free alternative when possible. Smart moves like that can vastly improve a training gymnast's diet.

little of something is good for you that a lot of it will be better! Vitamins and minerals don't work that way. And always talk to your doctor before beginning to take supplements of any kind.

CREATINE

Creatine is a specific protein that is naturally found in your body's muscle cells. When taken in larger doses than is found in the body, creatine has the effect of increasing the rate of protein synthesis within your body cells. What this means is that you will have more energy to exercise, and you will see a greater improvement in strength and speed when you do exercise. However, putting any chemical into your body can have negative effects as well, and you should talk to a doctor before beginning to take creatine. What's

VIRTUOSITY

more, creatine is only suited for adult athletes, so young people (those under the age of 17) should not take it.

PROTEIN SUPPLEMENTS

Getting enough protein from the food you eat can be difficult. Eating protein immediately after a workout is recommended (in order to refuel your body), but most people don't feel up to cooking or preparing themselves a meal immediately after a workout. That's why protein shakes are often a convenient choice. Many shakes contain blends of protein, carbohydrates, and fats, and some include vitamins, to help balance an athlete's diet. Furthermore, having protein immediately after a workout can help repair the damage sustained by your muscles during the workout. However, you should remember that while protein shakes are useful for supplementing your diet, they should not be used to replace normal food in any significant quantities. You can get plenty of nutrients from a balanced diet that cannot be replaced by artificial protein shakes, regardless of how fortified they may be. A nutritionist can tell you how to fit protein or supplement shakes into your diet safely and effectively.

Weight Issues and Gymnastics

A healthy body image is a vital component of a career in gymnastics. Teenage female gymnasts are the group of young athletes most likely to be affected by an eating disorder.

> **DID YOU KNOW?**
>
> *Gymnastics can have a negative effect on growth. At very young ages, there is little relation between sport and body size, but from puberty onward, researchers found that female gymnasts in higher classes suffer from stunted weight and height growth, probably because of their low-calorie diets. Some of these effects are permanent.*

VIRTUOSITY

The recommended energy intake for adolescent girls is approximately 1,700 calories per day, depending on height and weight and the amount they train. This is not dramatically far off from the average adult's intake, which is 2,000 calories per day. Coaches, parents, and doctors should all stress the importance of good body composition rather than low weight. Weight is an arbitrary number that does not have any real effect on performance. Body mass is much more important; having more muscle mass than fat does make a real difference in performance. The athlete that tries to increase performance by following a dramatically reduced diet works against this goal, not for it. Nutritionists have proven that muscle mass is lost much easier than fat when following a low-calorie diet. Dieters may believe that a reduced weight will improve their appearance, but they are sabotaging their career in gymnastics.

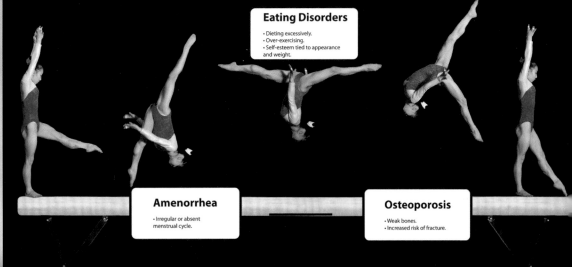

Some female athletes involved in "appearance sports," such as ballet, gymnastics, figure skating, and diving develop a syndrome known as "The Female Athlete Triad," which is characterized by eating disorders, osteoporosis, and menstrual problems.

Eating Disorders
· Dieting excessively.
· Over-exercising.
· Self-esteem tied to appearance and weight.

Amenorrhea
· Irregular or absent menstrual cycle.

Osteoporosis
· Weak bones.
· Increased risk of fracture.

Gymnastics

VIRTUOSITY

PRESSURE

There is an incredible amount of pressure on young women in American society to lose weight. A teen growing up today has an even more warped image of what is normal than teens did a generation ago. Because of warped media portrayals, the women's body images are negative on a global scale; only 2 percent of women worldwide describe themselves as beautiful. This pandemic of low self-worth is a serious problem that affects all women—but it is espe-

DID YOU KNOW?

Twenty years ago, the average model weighed 8 percent less than the average woman. Today's models weight 23 percent less.

Top gymnasts start vigorous training at such a young age that it can affect their maturation. For many world-class gymnasts, puberty will be delayed until they stop competing.

VIRTUOSITY

cially common among young female gymnasts. Female gymnasts are surrounded by images of ultra-skinny, rail-thin teenage gymnasts. Parents, coaches, and any other role models need to help teenage gymnasts maintain a healthy body image.

Gender Differences and Eating Habits

Gymnasts can start as young as five and most retire by their mid-twenties. Because of their age, gymnastic training affects a gymnast's maturation. Not getting enough calories can permanently stunt an athlete's growth.

Diet affects males and females differently during puberty. While female gymnasts are more apt to suffer from eating disorders such as bulimia and anorexia, male athletes often have the same unhealthy eating habits that the rest of the population has, including the consumption of too much fat. These eating habits can also contribute to long-term health risks.

This is not to say that male gymnasts are not at risk for eating disorders. Ten percent of male gymnasts will have an eating disorder, while less than 1 percent of the general male population suffer from an eating disorder. Being a gymnast is one of the factors that increase a man's chances of having an eating disorder.

Whether you're male or female, good diet is essential to long-term success as a gymnast.

Gymnastics

VIRTUOSITY

Cathy Rigby

Cathy Rigby, a very accomplished gymnast and actor, shocked the world when she began to speak publicly about her experience with eating disorders.

In 1968, she was the highest-scoring U.S. gymnast in the Mexico City Olympics. She won a silver medal on the balance beam at the 1970 World Championship, which made her the first American woman to win a medal on a global scale. Her talents were not limited to gymnastics; she also performed Peter Pan in a Broadway musical. Cathy was married to Tommy Mason, a professional football player, and they had two sons.

But not everything was going as well as it appeared on the surface: all the while, she was haunted by bulimia, an eating disorder. She told **People** magazine in 1992, "I wanted to be perfect in my attitude and in my weight. Inside I was going

VIRTUOSITY

crazy. I probably consumed 10,000 calories a day or more in fast foods. I can tell you where every McDonald's and Jack in the Box was along the way [to my voice lessons]—and every bathroom where I could get rid of the food."

How could such a talented athlete and actor keep such a dark demon secret for twelve years? Her story is a lesson to parents and coaches of female gymnasts: keep a sharp eye for warning signs of an eating disorder.

Gymnastics

6
The Dangers of Performance-Enhancing Drugs

Understanding the Words

Diuretics *are a type of drug that makes your body get rid of fluids by producing more urine. Diuretics have some legal medical uses: to lower blood pressure and to reduce pain from swelling and bloating.*

Amphetamines *are stimulants, drugs that speed up your body's reactions and processes.*

Electrolytes *organize the electrically charged particles that are in body fluids such as blood.*

Your metabolism *consists of all the processes that are constantly going on within your body.*

Stigma *is a feeling or mark of shame in society.*

VIRTUOSITY

Any substance intended to give an athlete an advantage over other players by altering something about his body is known as a performance-enhancing drug. Gymnasts most often abuse drugs that help them lose weight, such as diuretics and amphetamines. Gymnasts also sometimes abuse beta blockers or use blood doping.

Diuretics

Diuretics drain the body of liquids, which makes you weigh less. One of the most commonly abused diuretics is called furosemide. This drug can be used to shed water weight, and it is also used as a masking agent to hide other banned substances in an athlete's blood stream. The World Anti-Doping Agency has banned furosemide and other diuretics from the Olympics.

Furosemide is a veterinary drug used to prevent racehorses from bleeding and a prescription drug used to treat congestive heart failure.

VIRTUOSITY

The Roots of Drug Use

Why would someone who is naturally talented risk disqualification for a small boost in a competition?

Oftentimes, the source of the problem is unhealthy self-esteem that's built on the desire to please others. By the nature of what they do, gymnasts are encouraged to seek attention and approval from others: their parents, coaches, and the audience. Dominique Dawes, the first African-American Olympic gold medalist in gymnastics, told **Ebony** magazine, "When you spend the majority of your childhood surrounded by an audience, you tend to seek applause." Judges literally assign a number to a gymnast's performance as a sign of approval or disapproval.

Dominique, however, was able to grow into the mature understanding that you need to please yourself first. She stated, "No matter what you do, you cannot please everyone, and that realization has helped me deal with my self-esteem issues." She is now a motivational speaker, encouraging women across the country.

Gymnastics

VIRTUOSITY

Recent Cases of Diuretic Use at the Olympics

In 2009, the FIG accused the first Brazilian woman to win at a World Gymnastics Championship, Daiane dos Santos, of abusing furosemide. Dos Santos made a statement that she had taken diuretics to reduce her weight while her knee was damaged. She stated that she did not know ahead of time that she was going to compete.

Vietnam's Do Thi Ngan Thuong also tested positive for furosemide after competing in preliminary rounds of the 2008 Olympics and was suspended from competing for one year.

And when Olympic officials accused Alina Kabayeva of taking diuretics, she denied intentionally taking diuretics. The Russians' head coach stated that Alina took a food supplement called "Hyper," which contains furosemide. According to the coach, the gymnasts were taking it for premenstrual syndrome and had no idea the pills contained diuretics.

Diuretics are not the only prescription drug that is misused. In 2006, there were over 740,000 emergency room visits that involved prescription or OTC drug misuse or abuse.

Gymnastics

VIRTUOSITY

Many risks are associated with using diuretics. The fluid loss involved in diuretic abuse can result in diminished heart output, which reduces the athlete's ability to breathe and can hinder athletic performance. Also, as more fluids are lost, the body's ability to circulate blood to the skin and moderate body heat is often impaired. Other side effects include muscle cramping, exhaustion, and even cardiac arrest. Some athletes have died because of a loss of regulatory cells in their blood, called electrolytes, while abusing diuretics.

Amphetamines

Amphetamines are more commonly known as speed. They increase the heart rate and the body's entire metabolism, like a bolt of electricity that revs

Gymnastics

VIRTUOSITY

Young women in general, not just young gymnasts, are pressured by society to be very thin. Diet pills and stimulant drugs are a dangerous way to try and achieve this goal.

an engine. Amphetamines charge the body and mind and put them into over-drive. Gymnasts most often abuse amphetamines in order to lose weight, but the drug also increases an athlete's energy level, allowing her to exercise lon-ger and harder. The use of amphetamines during strenuous physical activ-ity can be extremely dangerous, however, especially when combined with alcohol; some athletes have died as a result. The drug's side effects include decreased appetite, insomnia, numbness, and heart problems, including heart attack.

Beta Blockers

Beta blockers are legally used to manage uneven heart rates or hearts that are over taxed. Some people, however, use beta blockers to manage nervousness during an important performance. These drugs diminish the symptoms associated with performance anxiety (pounding heart, cold and clammy hands, increased respiration, sweating, etc.), allowing anxious individuals to concentrate on the task at hand.

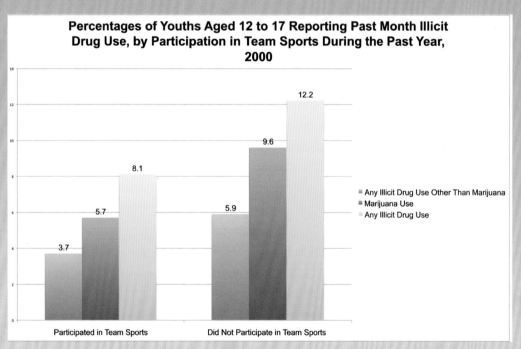

While some young athletes do try to enhance their appearance or performance with illegal drug use, this study from the National Household Survey on Drug Abuse shows that participation in sports actually reduces the drug use among high school students.

VIRTUOSITY

Beta blockers are not approved for this use by the U.S. Food and Drug Administration, and the International Olympic Committee has placed a ban on these drugs. Despite this, gymnasts may find beta blockers an appealing way to handle the pressure and anxiety of their sport.

Like all drugs, beta blockers have undesired side effects. Habitual abuse of beta blockers decreases endurance, which has a detrimental effect on training and performance. Other side effects include dizziness, rashes, depression, confusion, and coldness in arms and legs. Sleep disturbances, hallucinations, and sudden unconsciousness are among the most serious side effects involved in taking beta blockers.

> **DID YOU KNOW?**
>
> *Steroids are abused far less in gymnastics than in other sports. One reason is that raw power is valued less in gymnastics than in other sports like football or even baseball.*

Blood Doping

Blood doping is the injection of red blood cells or related blood products that contain red blood cells. This is usually done by extracting and storing an athlete's own blood well in advance of a competition (so that the body can replenish its natural levels of red blood cells), and then injecting the stored blood immediately before competition. The resulting unnatural level of red blood cells improves oxygen transport and athletic endurance.

Blood doping has been banned from athletic competitions. It is also a dangerous practice. Increasing the number of red blood cells in the blood stream makes blood thicker, which can also make it clot more easily. This in turn can increase the chances of heart attack and stroke. The blood can also be contaminated during storage, which can introduce infection into the athlete's body. This contamination can lead to sepsis, an infection that affects the whole body.

VIRTUOSITY

Getting Caught

The price of getting caught taking any of these illegal performance-enhancing drugs is very high. When an athlete achieves national or international status, and then officials catch him using performance-enhancing drugs, the results can be as dramatic as the loss of a medal. Drugs take away the pride of accomplishment and replace it with the stigma of being considered a cheater. Getting caught taking drugs can ruin careers that took years to build. On top of that, taking drugs is dangerous. It's simply not worth it!

The twists, twirls, bends, and stretches of gymnastics are an art form that requires great concentration, discipline, and many years of training. The sport demands that each gymnast be all she can be, physically and mentally. Ultimately, perhaps more than many other sports, gymnastics is also an art form. As gymnast Ivan Ivankov said, "It is through artistic gymnastics that I have experienced a lot of joy, pleasure, and satisfaction about my own physical abilities. . . . Those who only see the labor in my discipline fail to recognize the aesthetic component completely. This, however, is deeply connected with the human soul."

Gymnastics

Further Reading

Katz, Rachel L. *Gymnastics in a Nutshell.* Frederick, Md.: PublishAmerica, 2009.

Mason, Paul. *Gymnastics (Know Your Sport).* Sea to Sea Publications, 2010.

Mitchell, Debby, Barbara Davis, and Raim Lopez. *Teaching Fundamental Gymnastics Skills.* Champaign, Ill.: Human Kinetics, 2002.

Price, Robert G. *The Ultimate Guide to Weight Training for Gymnastics (Weight Training for Sports Series).* Sportsworkout.com, 2006.

Rose, Karen. *Competition Gymnastics Rules: Balance Beam, Floor, Still Rings, Uneven Bars, Parallel Bars, Pommel Horse, Vault, and Artistic Gym.* CreateSpace, 2009.

VIRTUOSITY

Find Out More on the Internet

Drills and Skills
www.drillsandskills.com

Inside Gymnastics Magazine
www.insidegymnastics.com

Sports Fitness Advisor
www.sport-fitness-advisor.com/gymnastics-training.html

U.S.A. Gymnastics
www.usa-gymnastics.org

Disclaimer

The websites listed on this page were active at the time of publication. The publisher is not responsible for websites that have changed their address or discontinued operation since the date of publication. The publisher will review and update the websites upon each reprint.

Gymnastics

VIRTUOSITY

Bibliography

All Experts, "Strength and Flexibility Training for Gymnastics," en.allexperts.com/q/Gymnastics-2245/Strength-flexibility-training-gymnastics.htm (12 February 2010).

_____, "Beginner Weight Training," en.allexperts.com/q/Gymnastics-2245/Beginner-Weight-Training-1.htm (9 February 2010).

_____, "Gymnastics and Dangerous Diets," en.allexperts.com/q/Gymnastics-2245/2009/7/gymnastics-diets-injury.htm (12 February 2010).

Body Building, "Gymnastic Training," www.bodybuilding.com/fun/how_gymnasts_train.htm (12 February 2010).

Diet.com, "Diuretics and Diets," www.diet.com/g/diuretics-and-diets (13 February 2010).

ESPN, "Amphetamines," espn.go.com/special/s/drugsandsports/amphet.html (12 February 2010).

Famous People, "Shannon Miller," people.famouswhy.com/shannon_miller/ (12 February 2010).

Gym Smarts, "Plyometric Training," gymsmartscommunity.com/blog/2007/06/23/get-maximum-benefits-from-plyometric-training/ (12 February 2010).

Gymnastics

VIRTUOSITY

Gymnastic Zone, "Training Safety," gymnasticszone.com/Safety.htm (12 February 2010).

Gymnastics Rescue, "Athletes with Body Issues," www.gymnasticsrescue. com/eating_disorders.htm athletes with body issues (12 February 2010).

Healthline, "Gymnastics," www.healthline.com/hlbook/nut-gymnastics (12 February 2010).

International Gymnast, "Dos Santos Tests Positive for Diuretics," www. intlgymnast.com/index.php?option=com_content&view=article&id=1237:dos-santos-tests-positive-for-diuretics&catid=2:news&Itemid=53 (12 February 2010).

Mayo Clinic, "Performance-Enhancing Drugs," www.mayoclinic.com/health/ performance-enhancing-drugs/HQ01105 (11 February 2010).

Media Awareness, "Stereotyping Beauty," www.media-awareness.ca/eng-lish/issues/stereotyping/women_and_girls/women_beauty.cfm (12 February 2010).

PPonlline, "Gymnastics," www.pponline.co.uk/encyc/gymnastics.htm (12 February 2010).

The Stretching Handbook, "Gymnastics," www.thestretchinghandbook.com/ archives/stretches-gymnastics.php (10 February 2010).

Gymnastics

VIRTUOSITY

Top End Sports, "Goal Setting," www.topendsports.com/psychology/quotes-goal-setting.htm (12 February 2010).

Vertical Jump Resource, "Ankle Bounces," www.verticaljumpresource.com/ankle-bounces-beginner-plyometrics/2009 (15 February 2010).

_____, "Standing Broad Jump," www.verticaljumpresource.com/standing-broad-jump-intermediate-plyometrics/2009 (15 February 2010).

Picture Credits

Gymnastics

Index

About the Author and the Consultants

J. S. McIntosh is a writer living in upstate New York. He graduated from Binghamton University with a degree in English literature. He enjoys making music on his laptop, playing poker, and being a literacy volunteer. Currently, he writes on topics ranging from military history to health and fitness.

Susan Saliba, Ph.D., is a senior associate athletic trainer and a clinical instructor at the University of Virginia in Charlottesville, Virginia. A certified athletic trainer and licensed physical therapist, Dr. Saliba provides sports medicine care, including prevention, treatment, and rehabilitation for the varsity athletes at the university. Dr. Saliba is a member of the national Athletic Trainers' Association Educational Executive Committee and its Clinical Education Committee.

Eric Small, M.D., a Harvard-trained sports medicine physician, is a nationally recognized expert in the field of sports injuries, nutritional supplements, and weight management programs. He is author of *Kids & Sports* (2002) and is Assistant Clinical professor of pediatrics, Orthopedics, and Rehabilitation Medicine at Mount Sinai School of Medicine in New York. He is also Director of the Sports Medicine Center for Young Athletes at Blythedale Children's Hospital in Valhalla, New York. Dr. Small has served on the American Academy of Pediatrics Committee on Sports Medicine, where he develops national policy regarding children's medical issues and sports.